Grandmother's Patchwork

Palewell Press

Grandmother's Patchwork

Poems by Jane Sherwin

Grandmother's Patchwork – Poems by Jane Sherwin

First edition 2019 from Palewell Press, www.palewellpress.co.uk

Printed and bound in the UK

ISBN 978-1-911587-28-6

All Rights Reserved. Copyright © 2019. No part of this publication may be reproduced or transmitted in any form or by any means, without permission in writing from the author. The right of Jane Sherwin to be identified as the author of this work has been asserted by her in accordance with the Copyright, Designs and Patents Act 1988

The cover design is Copyright © 2019 Camilla Reeve

The photo of Jane Sherwin on Page 101 and on the back cover was downloaded from https://tardis.fandom.com/wiki/Jane_Sherwin. No copyright infringement is intended

The photo of Jane's patchwork quilt on the cover and the other photos inside the book are Copyright © 2019 Kate Sherwin

The Leaf Collage illustration in "Watch how the leaves change colour" is Copyright © 2019 Vicky Cox

A CIP catalogue record for this title is available from the British Library.

Acknowledgements

Many of the poems in this collection have previously appeared in my self-published Chapbooks Nos 1 - 8. Some of the Chapbooks bear the same titles as the sections in this book: *No 1. Searching for the Numinous; No 2. Mermaids and other Faery and Fishy Tales; No 3. Gammer Sherwin's Bodkin; No 4. Marmalade: memories and mewsings; No 5. Joan Salmon a Tribute of Ditties; No 6. St Juthware and other Legends; No 7. Icons on a Journey;* and *No 8. Dame Partlet's Platitudes and Paradoxes.*

A number of the poems have appeared in Palewell Press's three Wordshare Anthologies (Wordshare being three female poets - Jenny Messer, Camilla Reeve and myself*): Poems of Water and Wonder; In Sadness and Solidarity with Suffering People Everywhere;* and *These We Have Loved.*

Some of the poems have been read at the Ledbury Poetry Festival, Rhythm and Muse, Loose Muse, the Amnesty Bookstore in Hammersmith and other poetry events in and around London. And others have been included in the various publications of monthly Poetry Groups around London, such as Loose Muse, Rhythm and Muse, Alison Hill's *Fifty Ways to Fly* and the most recent, Palewell Press's *Welling Up.*

Dedication

These Poems are for

MY CHILDREN:

Sam & Kate

MY GRANDCHILDREN

Danny & Ben & Tom & Megan

MY GREAT-GRANDCHILDREN

Liam & Kieran & Riley

Alfie & Isla

& Amber

And in loving memory of

MY SONS

Benjamin William (1965)

Daniel Zebedee (1965-2015)

And my GREAT GRANDAUGHTER

Scarlett Rose (2016-2018)

Contents

DREAMING OF WORDS	1
Reading the Qur'an	2
Fate	3
Class War	4
Archive	5
The Curse	6
Extended Warranty	7
Clutter	8
3.40. am	9
Composed upon Waterloo Bridge	10
Dreaming of Words	11
WATCH HOW THE LEAVES CHANGE COLOUR	13
Spring: Mid-February	14
Mid-April	15
May	15
Parakeet	16
Vivat Wysteria	17
Spring Quickens	18
Unopened Daffodils	19
Lenten Lanes	20
Forbidden Fruit	21
'The meaning is in the waiting'	22
Passchendaele	23
Kew Gardens	24

THE WATCHERS	25
Ants and Angels	26
Gabriel	27
An Encounter of Grace in a Garden	28
Merely Green	30
Anaesthesia	32
Stardust	33
This Sea	34
Butterfly Forest	35
Cape Town	36
The Watchers	37
REFUGEES	39
Refugee Poet	40
Advent	41
Asylum Seekers	42
Save the Children	43
Massacre of the Innocents	44
Tahir Square: 2011	45
Tahir Square: 2013	45
Tahir Square:	45
Birds	46
Belsen	47
Human Rights Day December 10th	48
Front Page	49

MOONLIGHT and MAGIC and TIDES	51
Full Moon	52
Violin	53
Mermaids	54
Song of Mami Wata	55
Flying through the Heliosphere 36,000 feet	56
Namaqualand, South Africa	57
Inheritance	58
The Earth Turns	59
Time and Tide	60
Moonlight and Tides	61
SEARCHING FOR THE NUMINOUS	63
I am that I am	63
Eastertide	64
Limitless	65
Homily from Hoo, the Holy Fool	66
A Net of Stars	67
Saith the Preacher	68
Heavenly Hopes	69
The Star	70
Wedding @ Cana	72
Maranatha	73
Logos	74

IN MEMORIAM 75
    Intercession 76
    Epitaph 77
    Whistler 78
    Daniel 80
    For Frances White, Poet, 2018 81
    Brubeck 82
    Scarlett Rose 83
    The Slate Blue Dress 84
    Harrowing 86
    Memorial 87
AMPERSAND 89
    The Green Door 90
    Mobile 91
    Tube Map 92
    White 94
    Goose Girl 95
    On the Silk Road 96
    The Witching Hour 98
    Cello & Birds & Bombers 99
    On Pondering the Carved Wooden Bosses of the Roof of Norwich Cathedral 100

POET AS CRONE 101
5 am towards Heathrow 101
The Curate's House, Clewer, Windsor 102
Easter aged 12 103
The Saga of the Sensible Woman 104
Megan 108
Remembering 109
Poet as Crone 110
REFERENCE 113
Biography – Jane Sherwin 113
Palewell Press 114

DREAMING OF WORDS

*'They flutter and chatter
Like birds in a flock'*

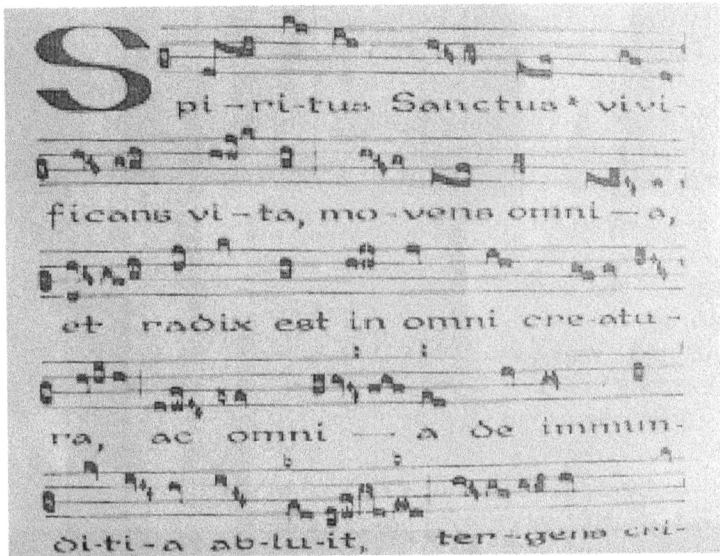

Casting one's mind back
to a particular incident
is like venturing onto a Möbius strip.
You reach what seems to be
the appointed place on the loop
only to find you are on the opposite side.

Through the transparent rainbow tape
you recognise the heretofore,
but none of the original emotion seeps through.
Lost in translation,
that initial spark
gives light but no fire.

Reading the Qur'an

I opened the Book, the printed book with this era's date
and I read the words
which the unlettered man
heard in the cave and took out to the world,
thus saith Gibreel, 'Recite.'

These were the words the 'rememberers' wrote
on leaves and stone,
letters in Arabic, consonants only.
those words spoke to me
down through the years
the hundreds of years
echoing others
of hundreds more years,
written on scrolls,
letters in Hebrew, consonants only.

Those lost vowels added by scholars
made English words that chimed in my heart.
Words that were printed,
words that were burned
and bodies too;
bodies and books burning in bonfires
the words of witness declining to die.

This brutal inheritance, once again
is new-drenched in blood.
The bigot not reading the Holy Words,
believing in rumours, seduced by conjecture,
imagines a Paradise ready for storming.
Whereas the lettered know the recital
is measured in mercies.
His mercy endureth for ever.

Fate

I have known love in many disguises;
deaths and adoptions and final betrayals,
but I came through them singing, defiant and free.

I loved and I lost, I gave and I gained,
I laughed and stood firm and I seldom complained.
I was girdled with grace and embroidered with joy
and was gifted a peace that is hard to destroy.

I thought that I'd build me a dwelling of dreams,
but the labour employed is not what it first seems.
One decides on a path, but is trapped in a pattern
that leaves on scant choice:
for the woof was long laid
and the song of the shuttle cannot be gainsaid.

If one enters the dance then the set must be closed,
one's personal fancies are purely supposed.
The Caller is Fate, the band and the beat
cannot be resisted. Rebellious feet
are captive to time.
                      The set must complete.

Class War

With acknowledgements to John Ball of the Peasant's Revolt 1381

When Adam delved
and Eve span
who was then
the gentleman?

Who the doctor
who the priest?
Who the lawyer
of deceased?
Who the butcher
who the baker
who, indeed,
the undertaker?

Who the Master
of Assizes,
who the shyster
in disguises?
What the causes
of the canker
that extrudes
the wanker banker?

When Adam delved
and Eve span –
a blessed time
'ere caste began.

Archive

My brain is addicted to paper,
in quartos and sheaves, portfolios, leaves
it flows through my house.

When I apply passport control
my liberal soul
shrinks from disbarring
that which appeals
to my liberal heart.

My liberal heart
is a sucker for stories
that pluck at its strings...
unbelievable things
that courage has conquered,
that love has defeated,
that death has transmuted
to truth undisputed.

A witness in words
seems to me holy writ,
how can I eject it?
The pages weigh heavy,
though light on my heart.
They trap me like spider-webs,
never depart
from the pyramid archive
I build in my brain.

And the papers remain.

The Curse

Hemlock, hellebore,
nightshade, belladonna,
henbane, aconite,
upas tree...
By these and the spit of the venomous snake
all that have harmed me
will traumatised be.

Pest and stench
and cancer and worm,
fungus and rot
and mildew bloom
slowly infuse the treacherous blood,
Erode the bone
and blight the womb.

Vomit and spew
and puke and retch,
keck and hawk
and sputter and spit...
but you , who have eaten my heart away,
will die from digesting
the fruit of it.

Extended Warranty

My mind is a rag-bag
a storehouse of riches,
of ditties and sonnets
polemics and speeches;
they lie side by side and conjoin in the dark,
give birth in the daylight, their issue...a spark.

My heart is a patchwork
each piece is unique,
the dark and the light, the figured and plain,
the hopes and the fears and the joy and the pain,
the pattern spread out, but the stitches unseen.
Its warmth and its shelter
are there to be used
its design and its colour
delight and amuse.

My body's machinery's
lasted quite well,
its hitches and glitches
ignored or well-oiled.
Though spare parts are difficult now to obtain,
'No call for them, Madam.
New models in stock
are faster, more complex and better design.'

But, what guarantee at the end of the line?

Clutter

'Declutter.' say the pundits
'Throw it out, buy new and trendy.'
'Declutter.' says my daughter
'it's going to be me, later, if you don't do it now.'
Fools, the lot of them, including my sweet Kate,
it has taken me a life-time to amass this little lot
and each piece is redolent of interest or charm;
Even the broken debris dug out of the garden
a tile engraved with VIC, the blue shards of a saucer
snapped stems of clay tobacco pipes
they all of them mean people who inhabited my house.

And I have added corals
from the seas where I was born
with pottery from Africa ,when visiting my brother,
and sequin flags from Haiti
and paintings and prints and photos and posters and candles
                                                and incense
and puppets and masks and peacock feathers
and glasses from Charity and china from Jumble and bangles
                                                and beads
and pairs of shoes that I no longer wear
but purchased from Biba , in a well-spent youth.

And, of course, there are books;
books in every room, books on the landing,
books by the shelf-full,
all of them singing ,dictating ,enquiring.

My house is an island
'the isle is full of noises' [1]
of questions and answers
and laughter
and love.

---

[1] The Tempest. William Shakespeare

3.40. am

The dahlias are blood and milk
in the dark garden: a sliver of moon.

The vixen screams.

blood and semen;
the catharsis of conception.

The distant sound
of passing traffic on the high road.

The slugs are immobile
drugged by the tartness of damsons.

The woman turns in her bed
the child murmurs in his dreaming.

The fox pads on his way.

Composed upon Waterloo Bridge

Slim spires of faith rise from the city's silhouette.
The buildings underneath often destroyed
by fire or bombs. Rebuilt, lest we forget
the will and trust and love they first employed.
These footprints of our faith have long been set.
Without their presence we would feel a void.
They are not empty, they are full of light.
Slim spires of faith rise from the City's silhouette.

'London Bridge is broken down',
Dane and Roman, axe and fire,
'Murder stalks in London Town'
(headlines before print was known).
Once more the threat of death's employed
and peaceful lives by hate destroyed.
Despite this horror and regret
Slim spires of faith rise from the City's silhouette.

Dreaming of Words

I am dreaming of words...
Words I have heard, words I have said,
words that I've written, words that I've read.
They bloom in the space
at the front of my head.
At the back of my eyes, they appear on a screen
projected in black,
the background is pale,
a sky above hills
with a rising sun.

Black and square, like the notes
of early plainsong,
black and crooked like runes,
or as lower-case letters, that throng
and that jostle.
They flutter and chatter
like birds in a flock.

As flower heads they float
in the meadows of morning,
suspended in space.
Then they rise with the sun
and mature in its warmth;
they scatter their seeds
on the breath of the wind,
a billow of whiteness
a sighing and sweetness
a longing and lightness...

I'm sleeping again.

WATCH HOW THE LEAVES CHANGE COLOUR

'Sweet Thames run softly I have sung my song.'

WATCH when Autumn tinges coloured hues
HOW hidden odours waft,
THE tenuous harmony emerges.
LEAVES late energy, a vibrant evening sun
CHANGE coats heaven and nature gleams exquisitely,
COLOUR chrome, orange, lemon, ochre, umber, red.
WATCH HOW THE LEAVES CHANGE COLOUR.

Spring: Mid-February

Will Shakespeare railed against the sere,
the yellow leaf, but this is drear
and little leaf, or none.
Bare hedgerows cannot hide
the litter at their roots
and scant are flowers,
mere clumps of modest snowdrops
or faint mauve of crocus.

The birds, at least, are tuning up;
moving in minims, blue-tits hop
from twig to twig.
But bare those staves,
awaiting blossom's song.
Fat pigeons tread like base trombones.
Seagulls and blackbirds, soaring high,
ignore the blandishments of sun.

Wind shakes the daffodils' gavotte
into a gallop.
Chill earth and shivering senses crave
warm airs from Spring's Chorale.

Mid-April

The satin petals of magnolia
fall on the yellow stars of celandine,
but, overhead, the damsons flaunt
their glory to the sky,
despite the pigeons' tearing beaks
and squirrels' depredations.

Slowly the furry budding of wysteria
firm up and colour in the warming sun.
They promise purple poetry to daunt
the faintly stirring lilac.

And visitors there are;
a butterfly, bees and a bumble,
a single robin and a long-tailed tit
amid the blue-tits.
Beneath the pots, squirmings of baby woodlice.
Tadpoles are squirming too, round in their bucket.

Not so welcome,
a mouse invades my house.

May

And now its May;
all blossoms gone
except the proud wysteria,
Who vaunts great tresses, blown by winds
and drenched by showers.

Amidst the grasses in the lawn
Will Shakespeare's golden lads all turned
to chimney sweepers,
globes of fragile, downy white.

Parakeet

There was a Parakeet
in the dark red tree;
you couldn't miss her
acid green against the dusky foliage.

She swayed gently
as the wind blew
holding on to a branch
with her left claw.

In her right she clutched
an orange nut,
which she raised to nibble on
from time to time.

Orange nut
green bird
aubergine leaves;
the suburban street
perfect
as a Persian Paradise.

Vivat Wysteria

The sun is setting:
thistledown drifts on the quirk of a breeze.
The rest of the garden is immobile,
in expectation of farewell.

Still prodigal, the garlands of wysteria
hang in the dignity of age,
their rampant flaunt diminishing.
Though a new birth comes soon again.

Theirs is a gift that flourishes in glory
at least twice in the season.
And, after that, strong suckers reach and clutch and strangle,
gaining new purchase for next year's extravaganza.

Spring Quickens

Spring quickens:
in the green loins of the garden
a freckling of celandines
echoes the yellow of the daffodils
that clump the grass.
Grass that till now
has lain low , cowed by the frost.

Spring quickens:
amongst the blossoms
little birds, small as new leaves, dart.
Whilst on the topmost branches
heavy-footed pigeons
tear with greedy beaks,
shredding the promise of this season's fruit
into oblivion.

Spring quickens:
the magnolia flaunts
its fleshy offerings on bare branches
regardless of the timid tardiness of leaves.
The sinuous foliage
of the rambling rose
flushed scarlet by chill winds
relaxes back to greenness
in the sun.

Spring quickens:
an elusive breeze is sweetened by faint perfume,
and a waiting world
trembles in expectation
of the fulfilment of daffodils, a carolling of crocuses
the incense of hyacinths
the kisses of primroses
the uncurling of the angel wings ,of the magnolia
and the blossom trees hymning heavy with birds.

Unopened Daffodils

There they stand, on the table
unborn
in a vase of water.
Their anorexic necks
and their pale, blind heads
could hatch out into
almost anything:
a dinosaur
a swan
a venomous snake.

Immobile
yet they peck
through their transparent sheaths
and emerge in frail virginity
awaiting the passionate kiss of the sun
to tempt them into flagrance.

Trumpets of silence,
they herald the Spring
and the triumph of resurrection.

Lenten Lanes

Lead me along the country lanes of prayer,
picking the wild flowers of my heritage.

Primroses lift clean faces to the sun
like little children, newly risen,
sure in their expectation of the Spring
oblivious of the cramping cold of sin.

We, who have trod this way before,
give us the grace to find anew
the freshness of our youth.

Use our salt tears as rain, to cleanse
the dust and sadness from our faces;
and bloom, as those sweet flowers
gifted afresh, as they have been
each Springtime of our lives.

Forbidden Fruit

My Father grew Victoria plums
'espalier' on the garden wall.
The sun warmed the stone
the stone warmed the fruit:
they waxed fat and tempting.

My Father was a country Parson.
He taught me how to fertilise marrows,
he taught me bible stories,
he taught me to appreciate Victoria plums.
He stood there at the end of a sunny day
with a look of admiration on his face,
'Coming along nicely!' he said.

I stood there, early one afternoon,
with stirrings of desire in my heart.
'Thou shalt not eat of the fruit of the tree of good and evil.'
I could smell the perfume of the plum,
felt a little trickle of saliva in my mouth,
I stretched out my hand:
the bottom plum was exactly the right height.
I picked the plum and I ate it:
the juice ran down my chin.

Later that afternoon my Father visited his Victoria Plum.
'Those dratted village boys!' he said.
It never occurred to him that his darling little daughter
was exactly the right height -
I didn't point this out.

There was an edge of satisfaction to my faint feeling of guilt.
Given the choice, Eve might have picked a plum instead

'The meaning is in the waiting'

R.S. Thomas

The meaning is in the waiting;
it may seem long and pointless
those cold days, without sun,
those barren days without leaf or flower
but there is meaning.

Unseen and burrowing
in the dark earth
Nature is creating Spring.
Without the waiting
Spring would not be possible.

Like a child in the womb
there is meaning in the waiting.
Like the formation of personality,
the process of creation,
the birth of a poem.

The waiting is not negative,
it is a mastering of forces,
an articulation of possibility,
a gathering of energy,
the formation of bedrock.

The meaning is in the waiting
for fullness and satisfaction.

Passchendaele

Water, earth and wood -
for the trees live no longer;
they are simply broken symbols
of desolation.

Water and earth are mud and death.
But the wood helps
to keep the mud back,
to build tracks, duck-boards,
to walk on.
Without the wood
the soldiers are swallowed
into oblivion.

We cannot live without water
but it can drown us too.
We cannot live without earth
but it can clog our breathing.
At Passchendaele
they could not live without wood.

Many died.

Kew Gardens

Kew is the green womb
lapped by the body of the Daughter of Time,
who lies in the arm of the cradling river.
'Sweet Thames run softly till I end my song.' [2]

The Monkey Puzzle grows there and the Gingko Biloba,
a species young when the dinosaurs roamed.
Banded in iron is the old Locust Tree.
The river mutters glibly of the aberration of starlight;
sweet Thames run softly, in shadow and in sunlight.

Cedars of Lebanon, Caucasian Oak Trees,
Chinese Wysteria and Tudor Hornbeam...
and over all, towering, houses of glass.
The river's suspiration whispers of the knife of ice
some million years ago.
Sweet Thames run softly,
singing of the wedding of the water and the earth.

We, who walk freely, savouring the blossoms,
bombarded by colour, diverted by design,
we are but ants to the Daughter of Time.
We are but grit on the bed of the river,
swept by the waters and lost in the sea.
Sweet Thames run softly, for short is our singing,
Sweet Thames run softly I have sung my song.

---

[2] This first chorus is from a Wedding Song by Edmund Spenser

THE WATCHERS

*'Every night they come again
To watch us while we dream.'*

Blue tits and piccolos
greet the dawn
with whistling anticipation;
clustering quires of recorders
like pigeons, swarm and plunder.

At midday, a chorale of oboes
herald the sun,
and hold it gleaming
till the evening shadows come.

Later, in the glooming,
the bass trombone slides,
as the sun
sinks into silent darkness.

Ants and Angels

'Go to the ant, thou sluggard,
 consider her ways and be wise.'

But beware, in this minute consideration,
that you do not miss, do not ignore
the flights of angels winging
in golden glory, above your head.

Ants are all very well
for town planners
and health and safety officials
and the often un-civil servants
that dictate our doings.

But, as for me,
I'd rather rejoice
in hedonistic happiness
with impish angels
dancing on the heads of pins.

Gabriel

Searching the morning orchard she found it,
a golden toe-print, left by the Angel;
not balancing on the metal head of a pin,
but on the tickling green grass of Spring.

So it wasn't just a vision,
a mirage of the sunlight.
He had been there, in the noon-day dazzle
positing his invitation.

She knelt to see the imprint better,
knelt in worship,
and was graced
with the gold kiss of a celandine.

An Encounter of Grace in a Garden

I was walking in the garden, late afternoon,
gathering up the washing spread on the bushes to dry.
My shift, when I wore, it would smell of rosemary,
my gown of lavender, my headscarf of sage.
The clouts that are used for cleaning and scouring
were bleached by the sun.
As I turned at the end of the parsley bed,
my hands warm with clean cloth,
my eye caught a glimmer, beside the vine,
I stepped a little closer;
the glimmer became a shimmer, became a glow,
became a Being of unearthly beauty,
became - an Angel?
'Rejoice, Mary.' said the Being,
'You are full of grace, God trusts in you.'
A speaking rainbow, haloed in light.

'Rejoice,' he had said, and my heart had leapt,
but then trembled in fear, for who was I
to converse with an Angel?
'Fear not,' said the Being,' God gives you a gift,
the gift of a son.' My tongue was dumb.
'A son to be called the most high, who will reign for ever.'
Then my tongue was loosed,' How can this be?
I am a virgin, untouched by a man.'
'The Divine will embrace you.
Your child will be called the Son of God.'
I closed my eyes, it was all too bright.
He went on speaking, his voice was gold.
'Your cousin Elizabeth bears a son, too.
She who is old is fruitful in age.
The promise of God is always fulfilled.'
I bowed my head and looked up through my tears,
'I belong to my God, body and soul,
I will do what he wills.'

His smile smote my face like a shaft of sun.
Then he was gone, and I was alone,
But a warmth of light shone through my flesh to my bone.

Merely Green

Flowers first appeared 130 million years ago:
Darwin

There were no flowers in Eden
merely green.
Trees, bushes, grasses,
no nodding blossoms, no shy daisies,
merely green.
Insects and birds no gaudy wings,
male animals no proud advertisements,
no flaunting colour,
merely green.

The apple was a joke.
Was it God's or Satan's?
One of them was trying to prove a point.
The survival of the species
needed to be more fun.

Eve saw the apple.
Any woman with guts
is up for a bit of provocation.
'If you eat of the Tree
of the Knowledge of Good and Evil
you shall surely die.'
The proclamation had been made
(though it was a lie)
by God or by Satan?

As she stood, considering,
this little green worm lisped,
'Tush, ye shall not die. [3]
If you eat the apple you will surely know
the answers to all the questions posed
by God and Satan.'
Paradise, when merely green,
can get a bit boring
after a while.

It was worth a toss of the dice
thought Eve
Death or Omnipotence?
Of course, what she got
was Sex.

So, was it God or was it Satan?
Maybe they are the two faces
of the same Being
(having a bit of a laugh).

Whichever,
Eve's decision led
to flowers and colours
butterflies' wings
peacocks' feathers
lions' manes
deer's antlers
and fun.

It's when you're old,
not merely green,
that you realise
what fun it was.

---

[3] Tyndale's translation

Anaesthesia

Drifted by sleep
the maidens stand
on the shoreline of dreams.

Pre-Raphaelite pale
they sway in the breeze,
their garments flutter.

In paint or in glass
they are taken for angels,
the passive type,
who stand around gazing.
My angels inhabit
a zone of fire.

These damsels portray
the fears that ignited
my girlhood psyche,
and the wimpish dread
of an ageing body
They stare out of the mist
with entreating eyes,
white arms outstretched -
arms waiting to drown me.

I must summon up my blood
for a clarion call
to my angels of fire.

no drowning for me -
I intend to depart
to a roll of drums.

Stardust

*'Vanity of vanities saith the Preacher,
dust thou art, and to dust you shall return.'*

But that dust
is the death of stars.
We are born of this death
and in our veins
primordial seas
tide their salt promises
of life.

Liquid in those veins
the glamour of the starlight
pulses;
articulates imagination
and desire.

Once the pulse dies
all that remains
is a handful of dust
and words upon paper.

'The dust returns to the earth, as it was,
and the Spirit returns unto God who gave it.'

This Sea

This sea, in which I float
which sustains me,
at whose margins I disport myself
in whose waters I refresh myself.

This sea, whose horizons carry my dreams,
where life was first formed,
this sea as it beats upon different shores
is given different names
but yet remains the same sea.

This sea, which changes its dimensions,
which erodes cliffs
invades fen-lands
recedes into the distance, leaving habitations beached,
this sea which once lapped the fastness of the Himalayas
now inundates the cities of the coasts
and floods up river deltas.

This sea, which divides and yet unites
is universal, despite its changing names
and bears the all-embracing one
of God.

Butterfly Forest

You must follow the Guide
believe in him, trust,
as he leads you deeper into the forest;
he says there are butterflies.
All you can see are a crowding of trees
that gets darker and darker,
and your disbelief grows stronger and stronger,
so that when he stops, with a curious smile,
you don't smile back, for all around
 are just sombre leaves, hanging.

But he claps his hands
and a second later those velvet leaves stir;
they are all butterflies, heavily sleeping.
They flap and they waken and soar into glory,
whirl upwards and sideways
changing the glade to a mazy kaleidoscope;
stir in your brains
dance in your veins
till slowly they sink, and they settle and sleep again,
leaving you yearning for Paradise.

Cape Town

The constant thunder of waves breaking
and the relentless surge of the endless and eternal sea;
these were the background of my dreams last night,
as I slept in a white bed
in a white room, shutters open,
perched above neolithic rocks
on this foreign shore.

Last evening the sun sank into the horizon;
glittering on pale cloud and dark water,
staining the wide sky
with vivid rainbow glory,
while little puffs of dark
floated in the glowing shell of heaven.

The young men talked of space travel and endurance
and the inevitable destruction of our world.

The Watchers

Along the quiet streets,
in the cold wash of the moon,
Angels
tall as church steeples
stand silent,
wings folded.

When night is over
and dawn pinks the sky
they will fade into their feathers
in the chill wind.
You can see them go,
if you wake early,
skimming high and fast
as the sun eats up the dark.

Every night
they come again
to guard us whilst we dream.

REFUGEES

'We must do more than weep'

The butterfly Hope
batters its wings
in a black box.

Refugee Poet

He is a poet
but he has lost his language,
his mother-tongue.

Pray for him Shakespeare,
John Donne, Keats.

Those first words he stuttered
baby songs he uttered
staggering around his mother's knee.
Those polished syllables
heard by his school-masters
University professors.
His first verse:
learning to speak
in his unique
voice...

All are lost
along with that mother,
father, brother,
grandparents, sister.

Pray for him as he crafts anew
another voice.
And surely, one day,
another family too.

Advent

Advent is coming:
The tears of Rachael and Hagar
Mingle with the weeping of November rain,
Weeping for the children who are no more.

Those who have died
Of famine, disease or war.
Those whose childhood has died
Trafficked, imprisoned, abused.

The leaves flutter down
Like the feathers of despairing Angels,
'Peace on earth.' they whisper
'Will it ever be?'

In the cold night sky
The full moon,
The pregnant womb of the Madonna,
Is haloed with calm.

Asylum Seekers

From the far corners of the map they come
fleeing unimaginable horrors
from places with unpronounceable names:
a tsunami of terror.

My sons, your daughters, our grandchildren,
stumbling, bewildered,
hungry, crying:

Nobody speaks their language
nobody knows their name,
they are shouted at, shoved,
crammed into lorries to suffocate,
set adrift in dinghies to drown.

Across the dotted lines of unknown countries
they are shuttled,
beached, at the break of dawn
on islands of mist.
The past is disaster
the present pain
the future fraught.

A miasma of nightmare:
my sons, your daughters, our grandchildren,
will they ever awake to sanity?

Save the Children

He sleeps on the floor of Dhaka's train station
on a double-page spread of the Bangladesh Times,
Discarded, once read, by Haris Kermodi,
as he left for his office, to wheel and to deal.
The rest of the paper is being used too:
a batch of small children asleep in the dust.

What do they dream of?
Faraway families where they were loved?
faraway families where they were beaten?
Parents who died? Mothers in childbirth,
fathers in accidents, working all hours,
taking short-cuts that ended in tragedy?

Maybe the sun and the shade of the trees
now left behind. The song of the birds,
the kiss of the breeze. The odour of curry:
the feel of a belly that's satisfied, full.
Maybe a future where they will be happy,
sleep in the warm, get work and earn money.

Haris Kermodi, discarding his paper,
bought fresh every day, gives never a thought
to the fate of these children on Dhaka's train station,
in Mumbai, Kolkata...
Lives of no value, like yesterday's paper,
lives that are taken by rapists and traffickers.

Yesterday's paper, crumpled and useless,
thrown down in the gutter
or blown by the wind...
the wind has no name,
no history, future...
nor have those children in Dhaka's train station.

Massacre of the Innocents

One part of the world rejoices
in exaltation at the Saviour's birth.
But, through the ages,
the refugee, the homeless and the destitute
sit in the dust, keening for their loses.

The massacre of the innocents
in Galilee, in the charnel houses of the Third Reich,
in the streets of Syria, of South Sudan, of Gaza
implode in a dereliction of hope that sets the stars to weeping
and the sun
to veil its eye
at these epiphanies of evil.

The child in every generation,
in every race, in every culture
is the innocent
and the future.

"Suffer little children to come unto me."
is an invitation
that cannot be denied
if we are to contemplate
the continued sanity of the human race.

Tahir Square: 2011

The name came to symbolise Revolution, Evolution.
'Occupy' at St Paul's Cathedral
took the name and pasted it up in a place of honour.
Tahir Square:
sisters and brothers united,
with their new technology in a new millennium.

Tahir Square: 2013

the circles of hell:
80 lone women, each stripped of her clothes,
by the desecrating hands of dozens of men,
thrown to the ground and raped.
If this is evolution it is going backwards.

These are educated women, but not yet emancipated.
Perhaps the male mob are the underdogs
eager to spoil another man's 'property'?
Certainly they want to enjoy their virgins
without the trouble of committing suicide.
And Eve is being blamed all over again,
'The woman, Effendi, she tempted me!'

Tahir Square:

sisters, we hear you.
The G8 have outlawed rape as a Weapon of War.
But how do you legislate against
lust and envy and greed and revenge?
How do you change a society from the bottom up?

Desmond Tutu says,
'Like eating an elephant - bit by bit.'

Birds

Along the terrace roof-ridges the birds are clustering.
It is a primal instinct to gather and migrate
when weather is contrary,
when food is scarce,
when danger threatens the life of the tribe

Across our world the poor trek;
fear, hope and desperation all drive them,
their destination the Shangri-La
on the far side of the next mountain,
the next stretch of water.

Unlike the birds, they carry baggage;
children too young to take wing on their own,
the old and sick, who do not simply die under hedgerows,
the prejudices that will fire anew
distrust and enmity in new generations.

Politicians pronounce and fulminate
in International Fora,
humanitarian workers solicit charity and aid.
the person on the Clapham omnibus
Feels a pang of pity.
Today's rubbish-bins are cluttered
with yesterday's newspapers.

Belsen

Birds do not live around Belsen;
even now, 73 years later, they are absent,
the trees and hedgerows are all silent,
Pre-warned by the same inherent instinct
that takes them winging safely over half the globe
year after year.

As they would flee a tsunami
they fled the coming Holocaust
of malice, brutality and suffering.
And for them, as for many human survivors,
the deep wounds of that trauma
linger.

Perhaps, viewed from space,
a loathly black swastika
still marks the map.

Are there birds singing
in the Rohingya Delta?

Human Rights Day December 10th

Born in Ghana,
James Kofi Annan,
(named for the Director General of the United Nations),
was sold to a trafficker
at the age of six
for $20,
along with six other boys.
What were their parents promised:
that the children would be educated,
apprenticed and taught a trade?
Or were they merely taken
in the settlement of debts?

The boys were employed in the deep waters
of Lake Volta.
Forced to dive
to disentangle trapped fishing nets;
nets that had cost $200,
ten times the price of a boy.
Four of the seven drowned,
(and doubtless were replaced).
Fortunately, at the age of thirteen,
James Kofi Annan escaped.

James Kofi Annan
now runs
an organisation which rescues
and educates
children sold into slavery.

Front Page

Aylan Kurdi, aged three
face down in the sand
drowned.
This is everyone's child,
innocence betrayed,
vulnerability violated.

Bigotry, ignorance,
enmity, malevolence,
brutality
backed by force and malice,
using weapons of mass destruction,
unchecked by world leadership
leads to devastation, horror,
fear and exile.

Abused by neglect and obduracy,
taken advantage of by greed and corruption,
unsupported by compassion,
thousands suffer
hundreds die.

This lone infant
is an icon
of the world's indifference.

We must do more than weep.

MOONLIGHT and MAGIC and TIDES

*There is more to the moon
than science will allow.*

Come with me to the edge of the sea,
there are seagulls crying.
In the shallow water, the ocean's
daughter, a mermaid, dying.
Dragged by the tide over golden sands,
her silver scales and the lingering strands
of her seaweed hair
lurch as the waves roll her out to sea,
judder and grate with the suck and pull
of an alien current, no longer home,
and twist as the eddies curdle and foam.

Full Moon

As an old woman
I am no longer ruled by the moon,
but I still bear witness to the tides;
and on full-moon nights,
when the water of the river
swells, pregnant with blessing
or destruction,
I give birth to dreams.

The golden circle of ice-crystals
makes a ring that weds the moon
to the silver glitter of the river;
as the one soars
and the other flows
in the cold quiet of the night.
And the stars sigh as the river tugs,
urging the flotsam to the sea.

For the sea waits,
slurring in drunken speculation
on the sands,
opening its maw to swallow currents
and spew them round the watery globe
making us one:
tempting the unfortunate
with impossible visions of hope.

Violin

The lonely Pierrot walks over the bridge
the bridge of sorrows.

Beneath the bridge the river flows
the river is deep, the river is dark.
But above, in the sky,
the stars are singing
singing the song of the Universe.
Pierrot raises his arms to orchestrate
the song of the stars
and they swoop in a stream
to the darkened river.

The river is silver
and flowing with stars
the river is silver
the stars are singing
the river is silver
the river is flowing.

The soul of the Pierrot
is happy again.

Mermaids

Dredged from the sea-deep of my psyche
are drowned mermaids;
girls of promise
with blind eyes rolled upwards
mouths pursed
against the whistling of the tides.

Strangled in their own hair,
stranded like seaweed,
they rise up from the ocean bed
to float
just under the surface of my mind.

Adrift in dreams
I bump against them
and, waking in the dark,
I hear their silent screaming...

I must acknowledge their deaths,
kiss them goodbye
and give them decent funeral,
weighing them down with adamantine stones
of opaque tears
and, thus bejewelled,
they will rest
quiet on the silver sands
between the rocks,
till little nibbling fish
pick them to coral beauty
with desire.

Song of Mami Wata

On her bosom she bore them,
Mami Wata;
from the coasts of Africa
to the Caribbean and beyond.
Seduced by greed and power,
the wooden prisons with sails
left the Gold Coast
and the Cote d'Ivoire
laden with grief and pain,
turning human beings into cattle.

Many were the bodies
surrendered back into her womb.
Mami Wata
turned their eyes to pearls,
their bones to coral
and their black curls into seaweed.
Mami Wata
sang her seductive song as lullaby,
rocking her children
into their eternal sleep.

When they sailed in the warm waters
of the thousand islands,
her living sons and daughters,
speaking a new language,
Mami Wata was reborn
as a beguiling, dangerous Siren.
She stirs up storms with the lash of her tail
and adorns her naked self
with cowrie shells and sequins of salt water.
They make offerings to entice her
and she swims into their dreams.

Mami Wata, Mami Wata,
she wanton dauta, La Siren.

Flying through the Heliosphere 36,000 feet

We are above the cloud layer.
Soaring through a dark blue ocean
with inlets and bays and seas.
Coasts of white sands,
shores of white rocks,
towering white cliffs
that build and stretch
into an ever-expanding distance;
and the sun, the sun, the sun.

A dark porpoise of cloud
comes snouting through.
The liquid air is cornflower blue.
With shorelines of fancy,
boundaries of dreams,
horizons of infinity
and, burning bright,
the sun, the sun. the sun.

The miracle of flight
treated as commonplace,
the wonder of heaven
blotted out by tiny screens
depicting TV games, old films.
car-crash orgies, gunfire and blood.
ignore the voice singing,
like a gnat in the ear,

'O the sun, the sun, the sun.'

Namaqualand, South Africa

We drive through the free-ways of the city,
out along the straight roads of the Western Cape.
Sea thundering, way beyond the dunes, to our left,
then the great lagoon, to our right.

At first, nothing but scrub on either side,
then tiny white daisies, smaller than usual,
crowding the verge, spreading away.
Clumps of shiny buttercups, patches of paler yellow,
stretches of bright orange marigolds
seas of mauve, clashing delightfully;
Matisse run mad!

Up on the skyline outcrops of stone,
smooth, massive - cathedrals, fortresses-
rescued by Time out of the sea.
Nearer still, great standing stones, solitary sentinels.

Tortoises crawl, Ostriches run,
Ibis, feeding, rise and fly,
black curved beaks, as on Egyptian paperai.
Eland and Quagga stroll in the distance.

At 3 pm the flowers are starting to close.
We drive home, by that everlasting sea,
which manages to trick us into laughter;
stepping down onto the beach,
it suddenly comes in,
as we think its going out,
and drenches us.

Inheritance

It is the Celt in me that informs the Logos.
The runes of hospitality are engraved upon my heart,
the songs of the lone islands, high and piercing as birds,
echo faint in my brain
and the cold wind of the north scarifies my being.

In 1930, the islanders of St Kilda
left the homes that their ancestors
had wrested from the wind and the tide and the cold
and journeyed to the mainland.
They left a candle burning in each window,
each door flung wide
and on the table of each house
a copy of the Bible, laid open at the Book of Exodus.
A perverse people, taking a perverse comfort
from an uncomfortable God.

The Highlands that they travelled to
were no soft Eden, no warm Tropic,
but a place where Sowans is eaten as a celebration:
a delicacy made from the bitter husks of oats.
A place where stubborn self-denial was admired,
where frugality was virtue.
In France there is a saying that
the Scots are like petit pois:
tough to get to open up, but sweet when they do.

A migrant people who have made homes around the globe.
And hidden in the soul of each
a splinter of the great shard
of the Eternal Cold.

The Earth Turns

The earth turns:
the morning star winks in the early sky.
Those singing stars have added verses
to their song nine hundred and seventy-four times
since I was born
and time and time again
the moon has tugged reluctant tides
around the globe.

Yet, to me, this has seemed unexceptional,
my only surprise the dilapidations
of my face and figure
and, maybe, my mind?
I know only that my spirit has blossomed
down the years,
And, though niggling annoyances persist
to bait my patience,
my affability has expanded with my waistline.

The earth turns
and will continue to so
long after I am ash and dust.
The wink of the morning star
intriguing the children
of my children's children,
ad infinitum,
for as long as the earth turns.

Time and Tide

The waters of the river
ebb and flow;
swell with the mysteries of the moon,
race with the fullness of the Spring floods
seeking the sea,
never to return.

Our dreams and longings
echo its tides.
Our existence also
ends in the sea,
in the great ocean
of the unknown.

But the Spring rains
and the Winter gales of life
ensure
we never will run dry.

Moist with renewal,
awash with singing,
the waters of my river
ebb and flow.

Moonlight and Tides

The Harvest Moon
huge 'n low 'n yellow,
seemingly caught in a cage
tangled in the branches of a tree
already Autumn-shed of leaves;
looking like an illustration
from a fairy tale.

Closest to the earth its been
for decades,
pregnant with beauty
mystery
and promise.

And the next day's tides
higher than the highest Springs;
the trees along the banks
dousing their lower branches
in the water.

Moonlight and tides:
there seems to be more to the moon
than science will allow.

SEARCHING FOR THE NUMINOUS

*'The eternal truth, born anew
each time a person dreams of God.'*

I am that I am

What timbre of voice was it, I wonder,
that spoke from the burning bush?
One imagines the hollow whoosh of bonfire,
the indigo edges of flame flickering against the horizon.

Perhaps the voice was more of an echo
reverberating against eternity.
For who could bear to hear, see the reality of Yahweh?
Actuality would surely send one deaf and blind.

Enough to feel the cold blossom of fire,
smell a singe of Pentecostal promise.

Eastertide

Holy Week waits
at the turn of a page
in my diary.
And I remember
a past self
walking the Via Dolorosa;
experiencing the Word
(translated into so many different versions
 into so many different tongues)
made flesh, stone, dust
and sunlight.

We carry within us
our own crucifixions and resurrections,
our rain-soaked Fridays
and bright Sunday dawns,
but we share together
the breaking of bread,
the mixing of wine and water,
and the giving and the taking
of love.

We are forgiven our trespasses
as we must forgive those
who sin
against us;
trying to emulate
the lavish generosity
(pressed down and running over)
of our ever-loving God.

Limitless

We make God puny
with our rules and fatwahs
our rites and ceremonials
our ten commandments.
God is not a pet
to be kept in a cage,
or merely a strong deliverer,
handy in emergencies.

God is the whole
the holy
the limitless
without horizon.

God is the Universe
the 92 chemical elements, that glow
and are recognised,
stardust, making us
as well as the oceans.
The force that thrusts up mountains of limestone
out of the bed of the sea,
that erupts, sending primal organisms
soaring again, to the stars;
recycles everything, wastes nothing.

God is the ever-changing certainty;
the blind burrowing of roots in Winter
and the white and yellow flutterings of Spring.
In the generosity of present, past and possibility
God values every spark of life;
the one who nourishes and cherishes
and cuts back
to ensure regeneration.

Homily from Hoo, the Holy Fool

Male and female created he them;
pinching together the stuff of creation
between his potter's fingers.
And when he had done
there was just this tiny clot of clay left over,
tucked behind God's fingernail,
just a smidgen, just a paring.
God cleaned it out and put it by,
'Subversion.' he said,
'it may come in handy some time.'
And the morning and the evening were the umpteenth day.

Christ found it useful -
pricking the balloon of self-importance:
'Except you become as a little child.'
Placing with care the banana-skin:
'Whose image is depicted on the coin?'
Breaking the rules:
'Let him who is without sin cast the first stone.'
Dining with sinners,
washing feet,
appearing to women!
Christ went thataway...followed by fools...frenzied and fickle.

And when the day of Pentecost was fully come
did the Spirit endow them with dignity and grandeur - no -
they ran around like headless chickens,
gobbledegooking.
So all you prelates, pontiffs and parsons,
all you magistrates, magnates and merchant-bankers,
all you statesmen, scientists and surgeons,
all you lawyers, legislators and lecturers,
cast off your laurels...
Except you become like that banana-skin
you shall in nowise slip into the Kingdom of Heaven

A Net of Stars

Dredged from the Waters of Chaos
the great truths are best made clear
through Legend and Poetry.
The Logos glows with energy
but Dogma is sterile.

In a tent of sacramental unity
I saw a gathering.
Lit by the light of the candle of trust
were individuals
sustained by the sharing
of the bread and the wine.
The Wind of the Spirit
lifted the tent-flap...once...twice...
tempting us out
with a glimpse of the wilderness outside.
When we who were bold enough ventured out
we found ourselves on a vast plain.
Around the perimeter were similar tents,
from which advanced a multitude,
'The round world and they that dwell therein'
the people of good will of all the Faiths.

Converging into a greater unity they came,
under the singing harmony of the stars,
a net of stars, joined and conjoined,
a shining net
etched against the dark,
against the velvet of the infinite,
cast by the hand
of the One who Is.

Saith the Preacher

Now Jonah took a voyage;
thought he'd given God the slip,
but God created havoc
on that foreign sailing ship.
He was flung out of the vessel
in the wild teeth of a gale,
but the mouth that swallowed Jonah was a whale.
Yes - Jonah was swallowed by a whale.

The light was pretty dim
in the belly of the whale
(though he didn't have to swim
and he didn't have to bail)
and Jonah's voice gave vent
to his thwarted discontent,
as he sat there, in the belly of the whale.
Yes - he really had been swallowed by a whale.

But the compass star of God
made the whale change direction,
and sent Jonah back on track
to the original selection,
which wasn't very far
from the town of Nineveh.
And thereby hangs this tale,
when he was swallowed by the whale.

If you're ever feeling gloomy
and you do not know what's what,
God sees it all quite clearly,
its just you that's lost the plot.
So, try a new direction,
it may brighten your complexion,
and make a new connection, let's call it 'the God Slot'.
For the ways of God prevail.
Witness Jonah - who was swallowed by a whale.

Heavenly Hopes

Living in South West London
I look forward to a heaven
where there will be no sound
of aircraft overhead.
How dreadful if
archangels, winging in
(every 42 seconds, as the planes often do)
brought with them
not hallelujahs and harps
but the gurning of engines.
As for pollution,
not the odour of sanctity
but ozone depletion.

The wings of angels
and seraphim and cherubim
must surely be silent,
like those of birds,
and perhaps
all that Holy, Holy, Holy,
might be mistaken
for the humming of bees
or a susurration of moths.

I am hoping for a heavenly hush
or the 'one equal music'
of John Donne.

The Star

God in his firmament fixed a Star
for Jasper, Melchior, Balthazar
to follow its luminous path, so clear,
through mountains and deserts for over a year.
Riding on camels, whose arrogant faces
were smeared with the dust from distant places,
feet-pads churning the ancient ways.
Through chilly nights and burning days
came Jasper, Melchior, Balthazar.

      They came bearing gifts for an unknown child;
      a child who was king of a realm exiled,
      a child to be priest for the God of peace,
      a child to be healer, that wars might cease.
      They looked for the child in the royal abode,
      but over a stable that bright Star glowed.
      In a manger-bed was the newborn child;
      his mother said 'welcome', his father smiled
      at Jasper, Melchior, Balthazar.

The mathematical lines of Eternity,
from the Dawn of Time to the Inland Sea,
are laid by God, with great finesse,
with infinite care and tenderness.
So, months before Gabriel came to earth,
to prepare the Virgin for Jesus' birth,
the Magi three had sighted their Star
in the chill night sky of their country far.
And Jasper, Melchior, Balthazar
followed the Star.

But their journey home was a curious thing;
they were warned in a dream, that Herod the King
would kill the child, once he knew the place
where slept that child in his mother's embrace.
So, their return took a different road.
In cavernous valleys great rivers flowed,
and they had to pass through the winter grass,
Wiry and white and spare and sparse
as old men's hair. Had they lost their Star,
Jasper, Melchior, Balthazar?

And they were changed, those travellers three,
no longer the men they used to be.
Instead of cold logic's cut and thrust,
they had found Love asleep in the arms of Trust;
so on their return, that bright Star shone
in the depths of their hearts, and their cares were gone.
And through the years, still glowed the Star
for Jasper, Melchior, Balthazar.

Wedding @ Cana

They were knocking it back.
Quite a few more there
than had been expected;
for the Groom had connections
and the Bride was a stunner.

But the wine was running out
and Mary noticed.
'The wine is running out.' she said to her son,
in a telling tone.
'What!' he replied, 'I'm not really ready...'
She gave him a look, the way Mothers do.
She said to the servants,
'Just do what he says.'

And when they did
they had at least 100 gallons of the best wine
(you could never accuse him of being a cheap-skate).
'Take some to the Leader of the feast.' he said,
and they did, and HE said,
'Wow, this is good. Where DID you get it?'
And the Bridegroom hadn't the faintest idea.
But the servants knew and they spread it about.

Next week's headline in the Galilee News:
"Local Boy Makes Good - Wine"

Maranatha

Christ has died
Christ is risen
Christ will come again.

But how will he come,
in the Power and the Glory -
blaring of trumpets
clashing of cymbals
shouts of Hosanna?

Or will he come,
as he did to Mary Magdalen,
in the quiet of dawn
mistaken for the gardener.
This time to touch,
and leave finger-prints of Mercy,
claiming us as his?

We do not know.
But I believe
that the Christ will appear,
in the Fullness of Time,
to each of us as individuals:
speaking to us
in our own particular dialect.

Maranatha,
Come, Lord, Come.

Logos

'In the beginning was the Word
and the Word was with God
and the Word was God.'

It is that Logos, Lord
that I strive
to capture,
to nail to the page
and to articulate.

Pulsed in the veins
are the rhythms of the heart,
stuttering in the brains
the words that must be born.

Each of us must midwife
our own small miracles;
releasing into the ether,
into the current of thought
the eternal truth,
born anew
each time a person
dreams of God.

IN MEMORIAM

*Each and every loved one
is stitched into the Tapestry of Time.*

I have always been
a passionate woman.
In my youth I was
in love with love
In middle-age
in love with life
and now I have
a hankering after death.

Intercession

Pass softly, little friend.
Though it is a hard thing to die
and yours was ever a stubborn nature.
The fields of heaven are bright with joy
and there are many there who love you.

Let go with graciousness;
the voices on this side grate on the ear
but, after silence, you will hear
the laughter and the singing,
the voices of welcome
setting out to greet you,
to encircle you with harmony and peace.

Pass softly, little friend,
though we will mourn you
we, who love you,
will be glad.

Epitaph

She is gone.
Gone through the darkness
into the night,
into the Everlasting.
At the dawn of the last day
the little flame shuddered
and then was still
and there was silence.

The silence broke
on the day when we met her in the church,
taking her into the arms of love.
Her family of friends,
absorbing her essence
and giving out
glitter of tears
murmur of prayers
singing of hymns
chosen by her.

After the tolling of goodbye
her final bow
was held in a haze
of flowers and candles,
incense and bells,
mourners in black
and priests in white.
Old women and men
had hobbled up
for the sacrament,
but her coffin was led
out of the church
by a lad with a thurible;
clouds of glory
swinging farewell.

Whistler

Over the Common the boy ran
beside the brook
down to the pond,
the birds sang
the squirrels scampered
the sun shone
and the boy whistled:
not a care in the world
and the world all his.

The boy grew
 and became a man
cares grew with him,
 heavy and dark,
but still
at times
when he worked with his hands
his craftsmen's hands
he remembered the boy.

Up on the cliff,
 beside the sea,
gulls called,
 moles dug
the sun burned
his cares away
and the man
whistled.

Now that man is ash
grit in the river,
but birds still sing
squirrels scamper
and under the sun
his grandchildren run
not a care in the world;
and his mother remembers
her whistling son.

Daniel

The early dawn sky
was clear silver grey
with shoals of silver fish
on the horizon.

The English country-side
still lush and bushy,
though Winter's approach
sent little worming chills.

We left him on the hospital bed
looking younger than he had for years,
hair brushed back from his forehead
and a face without lines,
though he would have been 50 in 5 weeks time.
None of his laughter left
but a certain peace,
and freedom from pain,
care-free.

He who was once
my baby son.

For Frances White, Poet, 2018

You'll need to find an Angel's quill,
to dip in dew and write your verse
Upon the virgin sheet of dawn.

We, who knew you, loved your song;
And now the birds will hear, new-minted,
Those syllables of love and joy,
The vowels of wit and flowing cadences.

And, missing you, we'll tune our ears
To catch the echoes of your voice,
Lifted on wind and singing in the stars.

Brubeck

He lay in the bed;
his body rejecting nourishment, pain.
His mind rejecting stimulation.

But the music filtered through;
bringing him sensations of vigour,
ambitions, schemes for existence.
The soul had already gone under
drowned in the cess-pits of egoism
and self-satisfaction.

The music filtered through;
persuading the body that it still had a future,
that the soul still had wings,
that the mind was capable of hard-wiring dreams.
Though the breath hardly raised the fabric of his t-shirt,
and the heart could be seen as a mere flutter.

The music filtered through;
like the lullaby
 that sings a child to sleep,
like the breath of a satisfied lover in his arms,
like the relaxation of the body after labour,
like the satisfaction of a job well done,
like a sigh of completion.

the music filtered through----

Scarlett Rose

Little angel child, you have learned to speak and walk.
Now, in heaven, you will learn to sing and dance;
and a loving grandfather will hold you in his arms
when you grow sleepy.

There, the sun will shine without burning,
Never rain-storms, but the gentle dew of dawn.
You will never be hungry or thirsty,
never be lonely or in pain.

Little angel child, you are truly blessed
and so are we, who say 'goodbye' –
just for a while – we will meet again.

The Slate Blue Dress

I bought the dress for dancing
and sophisticated 'drinks',
light slate blue, with fish tails,
and subtly self-embroidered.
        I wore it out to parties and
        I wore it to a wedding,
        where I danced, at last, a dance
        to say farewell to youth;
        a dance that had no sadness
        as I waved goodbye.

I wore it to a funeral;
she was my sister-cousin,
our children ran on beaches
and swam the sea together.
Each Boxing Day we volunteered
to do the washing-up,
to give us time for chatting,
whilst others watched the kids.

I wore it to the funeral of
an adolescent flame
who drove an open Bentley
and did a Bertie Wooster,
in the days when we imagined
that summer was forever.

Then I wore it to a funeral,
my light slate blue with tails,
the others had been older
but this one was my son.
Neither dress nor I had ever dreamed
that such a day would come.
      But slate blue is adaptable,
      it takes life in its stride,
      so maybe I will wear it when
      my dance and I have died.
      And lie in state enfolded in
      my slate blue dress of pride.

Harrowing

The ancient harrow, with iron teeth,
is still the way to break the soil,
let loose the dead, the damned from Hell.

Spring is kinder, allowing shoots
to spear through easily, its tears sufficing
 to melt earth's frost.

Those long-dead are loath to resurrect,
they have become accustomed to their sleep.
Breaking alive will be painful, messy.

As for new living, who would wish
to endure again the trauma of being:
learning to walk, talk, love, endure,

Only to topple, once again, into the grave.
Resurrection is recommended solely for those
with a capacity for outwitting pain.

Memorial

When those whom we love die
they stay with us always.
Divided, we yet remain interwoven,
part of the pattern of being.

In the chill of dawn
as we awaken
they come back to us.
They smile with us in the dusk
of humming summers,
laugh in the rain
and shout against the bluster of the sea.

In the dimensions beyond our knowing
they cluster,
to return in secret,
in surprise,
in sudden joy.

My sister still shines,
a single poppy in a field of wheat;
my father,
in the rash fullness of the moon
sailing, serene, out from behind the clouds.

Each and every loved one
is stitched into
the Tapestry of Time;
is interleaved
into the Landscape of Space,
and throbbing in the notes
that hymn Eternity.

AMPERSAND

*XYZ and ampersand
each wished for a piece in hand.*

The aerials on the roof ridges
and the telephone wire across my bedroom window
are the stage-settings for the acrobatics of the birds.
The great blank sheet of dawn
the diorama for their feats of fly-past ballet.

The Green Door

The green door is the door to my heart,
Knock and it shall be opened to you.
Leave it ajar for the sun to stream in,
but do not worry me foolishly
with babbles of lies and cunning talk
to rob me of peace and quietude.

Post to me messages from afar,
or invitations to celebrate.
If you need help I will come to you,
if you need comfort, welcome you in.
Food for the hungry, drink for the dry,
laughter and merriment, sermons and songs.

Green is the colour of everyday.
Green makes the grass
and the leaves on the trees.
Green is the backcloth that frames the flowers,
green is largess, the flood of the field.

The green door is the door to my heart.

Mobile

Beware of the siren song
the curse that you carry;
the voice in your ear
the music that drowns
the ring that diverts your attention.

Be aware of where you are
of the people around you
the noise and the silence
the state of the weather
the sun or the shower
the bird or the flower.

you must observe
with the credulity of children
the perception of adults
and the knowledge of death.

Be aware
time flows
blood beats,
laughter ripples
and laps connections.
You only live once
'you never step into
 the same river twice.'[4]

Beware of the siren song
the curse that you carry
drowning the present.

---

[4] Heraclitus

Tube Map

'Life is a journey, not a destination.'
But there's no point going round and round
on the circle line
hoping for revelation.
You need to change
at the interchange,
or even connect
with National Rail,
Riverboat Services or Tramlink.

You need to explore
the possibilities
of Gallions Reach
or Mudchute.
The bird sanctuaries
of Heron Quays, Canary Wharf,
Ravenscourt Park or Cockfosters.

The haunts of the Black Friars,
the Infanta of Castile
and Mary the Good.
Take the Auld Gate
to the White City.
Stroll around Colliers Wood,
or the Norman ones at Theydon Bois
and alongside Tooting Bec.

As for Gants Hill!
I went there once
and it was totally flat
for miles around.
A typo, I reckon,
should be Gnats Hill.

At Shepherds Bush
a sign for a knees up;
'Good wine needs no bush.'
said Shakespeare,
but the house
where the beer is on tap
is taking no chances.

However,
be careful how you meet
your Waterloo.

And, after life's experiences,
good and bad
then you can truly say,
'This train terminates here.'

White

Two clean sheets on a stiff-hipped bed.
'Now lay you down, Lord Randal.' she said,
'For the sky is grey in the gutter of the street,
so lay you down, rest your weary feet.'
The unbroken scream of the twisted stair
is caught in the caul of her tangled hair.

Two clean sheets on a black-boned bed.
'Now lay you down, rest your heavy head.
The beacons blink in the wall-eyed street,
so lay you, listen to your red blood beat.
There are rampant dreams at the black night's pane
that snuffle and snort in the whinnying rain.'

Two clean sheets on a stiff, stark bed.
'Now lay you down, with your limbs of lead.
The dog that died on that startled stair
has left his howl in my strangling hair.
At Lord Randal's feet must he mangled lie,
for my masters deed that a man must die.'

Goose Girl

Under the gold gown of the Princess
she still wears
the well-washed rags
of the wandering Goose Girl.

Upon occasions of state,
with diamond tiara and fox-fur stole
she parades in the great hall,
a woman of destiny.

But upon disrobing,
when her golden garment
shimmers to the floor,
she remains the Goose Girl.

Does she still long for
the dewdrops of dawning,
the flight of the owl
in the moon-bright sky?

Under her coverlet
secretly mourning
the times that she danced
in the shadows of night?

Only the Prince knows...
he alone sees her
naked of all
defenceless and true;

whispering secrets
soft as the starlight,
laughter and promises
bind them anew.

On the Silk Road

On the Silk Road
where rumours of Xander's fame still linger,
'He was here but yesterday.'
'He may be coming through again -
tomorrow.'

On the Silk Road
a Persian Garden is a dream of Paradise.
On the dry hillside, in the empty dust,
the seldom rains awake
the seeds of bygone Springs
into an instant burgeoning,
a flaunting passion that will lose its petals
in a blink of time
and fall again.
        On the Silk Road
        there are ruined shrines
        to ancient Deities
        the world has long forgotten.
        Little lizards flick their tails
        and disappear into cracks
        to ruminate on broken texts,
        and ants obey the unheard bells
        of summoning.

On the Silk Road
in chilly nights owls call
and swoop
delivering sudden death;
the scrabbling ghosts of myriad mice
clutter the feet of brave Xander's
soldiers, marching still,
at his command,
to dreams of glory.

On the Silk Road
nothing is changed, everything certain
to end in deaths that echo on,
and births unregistered as clouds of dust
blown by the winds of destiny,
obscuring landscapes of the living
as the eye blinks,
the heart stops,
the breath ceases...on the Silk Road.

The Witching Hour

I am pregnant with dreams.
Songs quicken in my brain,
stir in the darkness, biding their time.

To what end do my fantasies grow
Blundering like bumble bees,
knocking against the windows of my soul?

By what was I impregnated?
What passion tumbled me?
What seed was sown?

Will I recognise the features of my ravisher,
when these dreams are born?

Cello & Birds & Bombers

A retired cellist moved out of town, to a house in the country.
A house with a large and beautiful garden.
One sunny evening she took her cello into the garden
and played.
After a while she was aware
of birds gathering, birds singing -
all the while that she played
the birds sang.

The cellist contacted her erstwhile Producer
at the BBC.
He sent out people to record the performance - live.
The cello with the birds became a regular 'spot'
on Summer Sunday evenings.
Come World War Two
the live recordings went on -
a peaceful respite in a world of war.

Then came the command. 'No broadcast tonight,
We have bombers due in that area,
we don't want the enemy
 to deduce their destination.'
But the men with the mikes
 were down there already;
they made their recording, anyhow,
but it didn't go out live.

I heard that recording nearly 80 years later-
The strains of the cello,
the birds starting up,
a rumble in the distance,
a great thunder overhead,
then dying away
and in their wake
the birds still sang.

On Pondering the Carved Wooden Bosses of the Roof of Norwich Cathedral

They haven't got no navels, the likes of Ad and Eve.
Not that this lack disables, or hinders Eve conceive.
They've eyebrows, eyes and noses
and rows of rosy toeses
and bits and bobs and all that's needed
for the future to be seeded.

What a little squad of babies,
some what was and some what maybes
parents of the various races
filling up earth's vacant spaces,
till the fight for land begins,
round the clock and widdershins.

Grab and grapple,
stab and tackle,
beat and shatter
blood and matter,
bullets fired
and rockets hurled...
what a nasty little world.

Better turn the TV off:
    'this is the way the world ends,
    this is the way the world ends,
    this is the way the world ends
    not with a bang...

    But a cough!'

POET AS CRONE

Now, as Crone, the poet sings

5 am towards Heathrow

Tiny white clouds
in a pale blue sky
gleaming
like the scales of a fish.

Pearls
beyond price.

But already, lower down,
the horizon is criss-crossed
with the trails
of early aeroplanes.

Pirates, raping
the virgin dawn.

The Curate's House, Clewer, Windsor

It is Summer, the sun streams in
through the patio doors.
Not the hot sun of the recent tropics
but a glittering, fresh sun.
A pungent smell draws my attention.

I stand in the doorway and outside
my father is planning oak boards.
The wood curls, blonde and sweet,
catching the sun, catching my eye:
my first memory.

80 years later the table he made
is mine, family heritage.
The boards are the basis
of ceremonial, a secular altar.
And a place where I sit,
like a spider, spinning
the web of intentions
that is my life.

To be the child of a carpenter
has honourable precedence.

Easter aged 12

Even as the morning broke,
As each sleeping flower awoke,
Streaming from the heavens bright,
Tinged with sacred fire and light,
Ethereal voices seemed to say,
Rise up, O Christ. 'Tis Easter Day.

The Saga of the Sensible Woman

(In my 30s)
I am a Sensible Woman,
I have been all of my life;
a Sensible daughter and sister
and now I'm a Sensible wife.

At school a spot of rebellion
kept me from going insane;
but all that was left behind me
when boarding the homeward train.

My house is unreasonably tidy,
my paintwork unseasonably clean,
and no hint from my pleasant demeanour
that my soul is obtuse and obscene.

(In my 40s)
Yes, I am a Sensible Woman,
I have been all of my life;
a sensible daughter and sister
and now I'm a Sensible wife.

For years, as a Sensible mother,
I've laid out what's right and what's wrong;
taught love between sister and brother,
and the weak must be helped by the strong.

And now all the seed comes to harvest,
the chickens are hatched for the count:
and here in my hand I find nothing,
no pay to assay the amount.
But, Sensibly onwards and upwards
(though the head many be bloody and bowed)
I will march to the end, like a ninny,
unfulfilled, unhysterical, proud.

With tantrums the selfish ones win through,
neurotics suck sanity dry;
but 'good' girls go Sensibly helping,
whilst wiping a tear from the eye.
If you threw things, they'd have to placate you,
if you left , they might welcome you back,
but stay put and they'll use and abuse and
you'll drop at the end of the track.

(In my 50s)
I was a Sensible Woman
I had been all of my life
a Sensible sister and daughter
transmuted to Sensible wife.
While others were throwing their tantrums,
when others were tearing their hair,
I was the one they relied on;
responsible, biddable, fair.

But then came the day of disruption;
a wife was no longer required.
Our children were grown, and my husband
made hay as his sunshine desired.

I wept like a monsoon in Java,
heaped ashes and dust on my head,
drained bitterest dregs to the bottom,
lay lone in my marital bed.

But when all the weeping was over,
when moaning and moping were done,
I found just the one phase was finished:
The rest of my life had begun!
                              /continued

And, since I got kicked in the goolies,
my attitude's changed quite a bit,
I'd rather pitch tent down at Greenham,
than sit by the fireside and knit.
I'm still a dependable person,
still prone to be mother and mug,
but, when baby got chucked with the water,
I found that I'd swallowed the plug.

So, now, with incontinent ardour,
I indulge what my appetites crave.
And you'll find that this flaunting of freedom
will last to the edge of the grave.

There's no-one entitled to chide me,
nor dare to say boo to my goose,
constraints and commitments don't bind me:
this woman is out on the loose.

The sensible part was quite boring,
and I always last on my list,
but now I am free to indulge and
make up for the madness I missed.

(In my 70s)
I was a Sensible Woman
had been for most of my life,
a Sensible sister and daughter,
a Sensible mother and wife.

But living is full of surprises,
some of them good and some bad.
for love comes in many disguises,
and better to laugh than be sad.

Better to give than to miser,
better to squander than save,
'go with the flow' and with gladness;
wholeness belongs to the brave.

Cast all your cares out behind you,
relish bother plain and sublime.
Live every day in its fullness and
Dance to the Music of Time.

Megan

You are an icon of motherhood;
the one who is prepared to suffer
so that her child should not.

The one who stands firm
whilst the plates of the world
slide in confusion.

The one who sees clearly
whilst tears of incomprehension
Stream from her eyes.

The one who can give the kiss of comfort
when her heart is breaking.
The one who is Love.

Remembering

The gold has fallen.
Now stark branches etch the blank grey sky.
Scattered along the pavements
a wet golden hoard slips underfoot.

Waiting for snow, the squirrels' noses twitch;
they scrabble for lost nuts, to store away.
As we store memories in this fading season,
bury in our hearts secrets and forgotten promises.

Will Spring see flowers again? It seems unlikely;
it takes effort to pierce through the heavy clods of earth.
The kernel of expectation lies dormant, cold;
is it an embryo, will it uncurl?

Only the enticement of the sun will tell.

The last rose sheds
its crimson blood
petal by petal.

Poet as Crone

The Virgin Poet wandered on the dawn-bright shore
listening to the singing of the mermaids,
The wild wind lifted her hair
and filled her ears with sadness.
She climbed beyond the cloud-line of the mountains,
seeing the red dawn wake beyond the crags,
rode on the wings of eagles.
Down she came, into the verdant forest,
gathering flowers to plait into her hair,
languished in the rustling woods
yearning for the unicorn.

The Mother Poet crooned
to her tree-top babies,
knitting them nests of rhythm and rhyme,
crocheting strings of daisies and dandelions;
clocks by which to measure
the endless days of summer.
Answering the riddles
how many miles to Dover or Norwich or Babylon?
And where's that Old Woman
tossed up in her basket,
now that the moon sails
clear in the skies.

Now, as Crone, the poet sings
of yesterday's delights and dancing,
today's desires and longings
and tomorrow's dreams of peace;
not merely for herself and for her children
but for Humanity and for Creation.
For the green world spinning in the starry heavens,
the deep seas washing tides, draining rivers,
the cloud layer and the painted skies of dawn and sunset.
Within her lingers the Virgin's innocence and the Mother's caring;
she utters spells to guard and guide Earth's children
on their journeys to the End:
be it bang or whimper or soughing of stars.

REFERENCE

Biography – Jane Sherwin

Born in 1934 to a Church of England Clergyman and a Primary School Teacher, my poetic imagination was nourished early by weekly readings of the King James' edition of the Bible and singing hymns from the various poets who have enhanced our liturgy; Charles Wesley, Mrs Alexander, Christina Rossetti, Percy Dearmer, John Elerton, Reginald Heber, Isaac Watts, William Cowper, George Herbert et al. Whilst doing the washing up together my mother and I sang Folk Songs and Ballads. Later, at my Clergy Daughters Boarding School, those infusions were administered daily.

A voracious reader, I was much more interested in the Trojan War than World War 2. At 9 and a half I wrote a narrative poem which finished,
>With crimson pools of blood to pay
>The sins of those who'd stolen away
>Fair Helen of Troy.

That was when I found out that there had never been a female Poet Laureate. I was determined to be the first. I actually became an actress instead, followed by volunteer work for various good causes, including Amnesty International, Refugees and the Homeless. But poetry was a common thread running through all of these endeavours.

At Amnesty I collected poems written by prisoners or about Human Rights abuses and published a book called 'Poetry as Witness'. I also sought out Latin American Liberation Theology in translation and used it alongside my own prayers in my Annual Human Rights Day Vigil and other services. There is often very little difference between poetry and prayer.

St. Michael and All Angels, Barnes, is the church that I have attended for over 50 years and I have, from time to time, run monthly poetry sessions, such as 'Poetry as Meditation' and 'Healing the Planet'.

However, in my early 70s, having been pipped to the laureate post by Carol Ann Duffy, I decided to give up all 'good works', including housework, and just concentrate on the poetry. A decade or so later, here I am...

Palewell Press

Palewell Press is an independent publisher handling poetry, fiction and non-fiction with a focus on books that foster Justice, Equality and Sustainability. The Editor can be reached on enquiries@palewellpress.co.uk

Lightning Source UK Ltd.
Milton Keynes UK
UKHW020743110820
368035UK00007B/215